WIDE SLUMBER FOR LEPIDOPTERISTS

~ *a.rawlings*

COACH HOUSE BOOKS 2006

Published with the assistance of the Canada Council for the Arts and the Ontario Arts Council. We also acknowledge the financial support of the Government of Ontario through the Ontario Book Publishing Tax Credit Program and the Government of Canada through the Book Publishing Industry Development Program (BPIDP).

LIBRARY AND ARCHIVES CANADA CATALOGUING IN PUBLICATION

Rawlings, Angela, 1978-

    Wide slumber for lepidopterists / a. rawlings ; illustrations by Matt Ceolin.

Poems.

ISBN-13: 978-1-55245-169-4
ISBN-10: 1-55245-169-0

    I. Title.

PS8635.A938W52 2006   C813'.6   C2006-901136-2

for Northern Ontario

a hoosh a ha

a hoosh a ha

a hoosh a ha

a hoosh a ha

a hoosh a ha

a hoosh a ha

a hoosh a ha

                                                            a hoosh a ha

a hoosh a ha
                                                    a hoosh a ha
                                                    a hoosh a ha

                                                    a hoosh a ha
a hoosh a ha   a hoosh a ha

a hoosh a ha
    a hoosh a ha

                                            a hoosh a ha
        a hoosh a ha

                                                    a hoosh a ha

                                            a hoosh a ha
                                                a hoosh a ha

a hoosh a ha

a hoosh a ha

a hoosh a ha

a hoosh a ha

a hoosh a ha

a hoosh a ha

a hoosh a ha a hoosh a ha a hoosh a ha a hoosh a ha

a hoosh a ha a hoosh a ha a hoosh a ha a hoosh a ha

a hoosh a ha

a hoosh a ha

a hoosh a ha

a hoosh a ha

a hoosh a ha a hoosh a ha a hoosh a ha a hoosh a ha a hoosh a ha

a hoosh a ha

a hoosh a ha a hoosh a ha

a hoosh a ha a hoosh a ha

a hoosh a ha a hoosh a ha a hoosh a ha a hoosh a ha a hoosh a ha

a hoosh a ha

a hoosh a ha a hoosh a ha

a hoosh a ha

a hoosh a ha

a hoosh a ha a hoosh a ha

a hoosh a ha

a hoosh a ha a hoosh a ha a hoosh a ha a hoosh a ha a hoosh a ha a hoosh a ha a hoosh a ha a hoosh a ha

a hoosh a ha

O

figure 1

EGG – INSOMNIA

We descend on a field by a lake. *a hoosh* The lupin, sleep, the fog. *a ha* Fireflies, silent moths. We bury our legs in sand. Sound through sand is dormant. We desire sleep to enter, virginal.

We stretch our feelers toward the warm body. *a a* Slowly, hands fog-damp spin plants, form air-filled hollows, breath cocooned, fur soft and blurred, heavy even heavenly. *hoosh* Soft like quiet. *ha*

Soft like we quiver.

Slow light touch of hand on wing, scales brush off like butterfly kisses, hand on brow, eyelash dew and fog, breath and fur our entrance and we caress the dulled wet passage, the flicker of soft quiet like sound or sand, when larva eats its eggshell and becomes pupa *a hoosh*

we tongue our shell, our conch, we smell the honeysuckle sweat heavily in the night air. Heave. *a hoosh* The fragrance a push of belly against abdomen, tongue buried deep in the suckle the honey and the brush-foots wake and crowd, thrust or pulse, spastic praxis, massive pulse out of sync. This is not what this is no, we intended, we thought sleep and none came we come. *ha a a ha* Horned caterpillars epilepse, wood nymphs spin and hang crude cocoons

we hold our slow high flight

we are taut while we thrust against the inner wall. Sleep is bruised or screams or none comes but we desire, we feel the full hot flesh of our wing swipe grass, scrape sand, we push ourselves out of ourselves, into our sound our hand our sweet wet hot our path, mourn, rake, master or muster. Glisten swell come and the story's arousal, twenty eyes unblink when the sun's awake and even when it's not the brain speaks, screams, swells and huge battened eyes of a hundred hungry mouths, no moths, wait this will move. Will move to sleep not yet. Diurnal motion a heavenly body a soft steel wool. Diurnal panic or we come and the sweet hot full the electricity of our shelled wholes, our steeled wools, shocks us, lightning through our hole, up into the sand, we roll away from ourselves, breathless. *a hoosh a ha* We have five seconds of lightning and love like laid in plant tissues or in narrow slits or crevices. Soft innocent curving.

Laid in soft theta tissues or in narrow row innocents.

Laid in narrow tissues or in in soft theta curving of the innocence
of narrow issues; in curves of nonsense lie in no sense in soft curving rows
of tissue curves of of innocence narrow soft curves of innocence

laid in soft narrow curves of innocents, of issue,

figure 2

EGG, LARVA – DYSSOMNIA

Larva is a cage where moths bleed silk, sleep woven.

The cage a bed.
>   *Collect, kill and mount specimen.*
Three cages comatose.

These cages bled.

Catch specimen in aerial net.

Pinch thorax between thumb and forefinger.

Slide specimen into envelope; store in box with insecticide.

Inhale to sleep crows on crows of army worms; uncontrol cannibalistic owlet moths.

Relax dried specimen by placing in humid environment.

Welcome to the Centre for Sleep and Dream Studies. Welcme to th

Enter. Sleep nd ream. elcm

Use fungicide to prevent mould growth on specimen.

nether leap, the flights, coalesceTHE#FLIGHTSimplode, coal

flash and out. Welcome sit in the egg and gestate theory#gestalt cutworms.

When specimen is adequately relaxed, remove from humidity using forceps.

Hold specimen by thorax, and force insect pin
through middle of body between wings.
Pin specimen to mounting board.

Enter smoke and steel wool. Soft like stitch. Soft like flurry. Soft like grind. A caterpillar overtakes the bedrail, crawls beneath quilt, sheet. Crawls a line an inch a deformed and digested hymen. Eat flurry and grind. Specula. Larva silks itself to our throat,

weaves# #

    ## ##thing

     #thick

        ###as#thing

       # #########shantung#and#tussah

            #lungs##thick#sheets

            #of#lungs####complexhale

Manipulate wings simultaneously to avoid twisting body.
Pin wings to mounting board.

called by number

Pin wings near large veins to avoid tears.

Place paper over wings to prevent curling while drying.

pins through epidermis

a wall, a tooth

Place specimen under lamp to increase drying time.

tsniaga tsurht rotcelloc a#ŧilps#ŧips nehT

a moth with barbed spines

vulva, uvula

Keep mounted specimen in low-moisture condition to prevent mould.
Avoid direct sunlight to prevent fading.
Store in tightly closed box with insecticide to prevent dermestid beetle larvae
and book lice from feeding on body parts.

537neon. Account

for breath: slow, slow, quick-slip

slow and slow soft mouth with barbed spines.

Stretch muscle; pin leg. Chew waste or rest. Part

and partner lips. Push labial vibration across leaf,

across membrane. Spit dew. Spin waist with hand and in and

turn#HEIGHT#turn pulse. Pull body outside body. Moisten

ocho#THEFLIGHT#oco netso do edistuo ob llu .. eslu

rut#THE#ru da ni da nah tiw tsia ni .. arbem

sorca ael sorca nitar laibal

su .. ser ro etsaw

weh .. eni dera tiw tuom

os wols na wols ciu

wols aer ro nuocc .noen###

ti ur tor foknur

a hoosh a ha

rem nrem

                                                                    a hush a ha

                    a hoosh a ha
                        a hoosh a ha   insomnia cataplexy
    a hoosh a ha uh hush uh ha oh hoosh oh ha   a hookah ha
circadian arrhythmia
a hoosh a ha   instars ditrysia
        a hoosh a ha   a hoosh a ha   sleep apnea dyssomnia
            a hoosh a ha a hoosh a ha mm hoosh mm ha mm hoosh a ha
            or rush and a   a hoosh a ha ah hoosh a a
                hypnic twitch sleep spindles deep slumber restoration
                    a sh a ha   and sh and a and sh and ah
a hoosh a ha   a mmsh soma a hoosh soma a mmsh a ha
    oviposition oscillation dorsal nectar organ ectothermia myrmecophily
                                                electroencephalograph

~

figure 3

LARVA − NREM

tango to bed
        Wingbeats and heartbeats
over, extend, superimpThere
is a step, the Ocho, there
is a bed for Click of a switch
sleep Our eyes turn inward   arching
            collapse our eyes
a vaporous trail we leave behind
where we crawl legs and   ants
            legs behind us   like stars
when legs scramble over legs on
legs on thigh on a whole aura of
            electricity think
                lightning think hyperlove sleepspell myrmecophilust

story stars and starts itself. Thick in our sweat, repeat, collapse lunge no wait

Story instars think lungs in sweet thick or eat.

Story starts itself. Sweat, lungless, its lapped thighs, our instant rape, stir
the thick sweet colour of lungs in stars and elves. Think our or
self stored in reap and instars. Start

repeat and repeat

a hoosh
a tremendous crash

NREM remember REM remember MNR

is
is   a word
a word   is   comes easy
somnambulance somnambulance somnambulance somnambulance

xxx y zzz xxx y zzz xxx y zzz xxx y zzz xxx y zzz xxx y zzz xxx y zzz xxx y zzz xxx y zzz xxx y zzz
thorax y zzz thorax y zzz thorax y zzz thorax y zzz thorax y zzz thorax y zzz thorax y zzz thorax y zzz
cervix y zzz cervix y zzz cervix y zzz cervix y zzz cervix y zzz cervix y zzz cervix y zzz cervix y zzz
xxx y zzz xxx y zzz xxx y zzz xxx y zzz xxx y zzz xxx y zzz xxx y zzz xxx y zzz xxx y zzz xxx y zzz
thorax y zzz thorax y zzz thorax y zzz thorax y zzz thorax y zzz thorax y zzz thorax y zzz thorax y zzz
cervix y zzz cervix y zzz cervix y zzz cervix y zzz cervix y zzz cervix y zzz cervix y zzz cervix y zzz
xxx y zzz xxx y zzz xxx y zzz xxx y zzz xxx y zzz xxx y zzz xxx y zzz xxx y zzz xxx y zzz xxx y zzz
thorax y zzz thorax y zzz thorax y zzz thorax y zzz thorax y zzz thorax y zzz thorax y zzz thorax y zzz
cervix y zzz cervix y zzz cervix y zzz cervix y zzz cervix y zzz cervix y zzz cervix y zzz cervix y zzz
xxx y zzz xxx y zzz xxx y zzz xxx y zzz xxx y zzz xxx y zzz xxx y zzz xxx y zzz xxx y zzz xxx y zzz
thorax y zzz thorax y zzz thorax y zzz thorax y zzz thorax y zzz thorax y zzz thorax y zzz thorax y zzz
cervix y zzz cervix y zzz cervix y zzz cervix y zzz cervix y zzz cervix y zzz cervix y zzz cervix y zzz
xxx y zzz xxx y zzz xxx y zzz xxx y zzz xxx y zzz xxx y zzz xxx y zzz xxx y zzz xxx y zzz xxx y zzz
thorax y zzz thorax y zzz thorax y zzz thorax y zzz thorax y zzz thorax y zzz thorax y zzz thorax y zzz
cervix y zzz cervix y zzz cervix y zzz cervix y zzz cervix y zzz cervix y zzz cervix y zzz cervix y zzz
xxx y zzz xxx y zzz xxx y zzz xxx y zzz xxx y zzz xxx y zzz xxx y zzz xxx y zzz xxx y zzz xxx y zzz
thorax y zzz thorax y zzz thorax y zzz thorax y zzz thorax y zzz thorax y zzz thorax y zzz thorax y zzz
cervix y zzz cervix y zzz cervix y zzz cervix y zzz cervix y zzz cervix y zzz cervix y zzz cervix y zzz
xxx y zzz xxx y zzz xxx y zzz xxx y zzz xxx y zzz xxx y zzz xxx y zzz xxx y zzz xxx y zzz xxx y zzz
thorax y zzz thorax y zzz thorax y zzz thorax y zzz thorax y zzz thorax y zzz thorax y zzz thorax y zzz
cervix y zzz cervix y zzz cervix y zzz cervix y zzz cervix y zzz cervix y zzz cervix y zzz cervix y zzz
xxx y zzz xxx y zzz xxx y zzz xxx y zzz xxx y zzz xxx y zzz xxx y zzz xxx y zzz xxx y zzz xxx y zzz
thorax y zzz thorax y zzz thorax y zzz thorax y zzz thorax y zzz thorax y zzz thorax y zzz thorax y zzz
cervix y zzz cervix y zzz cervix y zzz cervix y zzz cervix y zzz cervix y zzz cervix y zzz cervix y zzz
xxx y zzz xxx y zzz xxx y zzz xxx y zzz xxx y zzz xxx y zzz xxx y zzz xxx y zzz xxx y zzz xxx y zzz
thorax y zzz thorax y zzz thorax y zzz thorax y zzz thorax y zzz thorax y zzz thorax y zzz thorax y zzz
cervix y zzz cervix y zzz cervix y zzz cervix y zzz cervix y zzz cervix y zzz cervix y zzz cervix y zzz
xxx y zzz xxx y zzz xxx y zzz xxx y zzz xxx y zzz xxx y zzz xxx y zzz xxx y zzz xxx y zzz xxx y zzz
thorax y zzz thorax y zzz thorax y zzz thorax y zzz thorax y zzz thorax y zzz thorax y zzz thorax y zzz
cervix y zzz cervix y zzz cervix y zzz cervix y zzz cervix y zzz cervix y zzz cervix y zzz cervix y zzz
xxx y zzz xxx y zzz xxx y zzz xxx y zzz xxx y zzz xxx y zzz xxx y zzz xxx y zzz xxx y zzz xxx y zzz
thorax y zzz thorax y zzz thorax y zzz thorax y zzz thorax y zzz thorax y zzz thorax y zzz thorax y zzz
cervix y zzz cervix y zzz cervix y zzz cervix y zzz cervix y zzz cervix y zzz cervix y zzz cervix y zzz

zzz y xxx zzz y xxx zzz y xxx zzz y xxx zzz y xxx zzz y xxx zzz y xxx zzz y xxx zzz y xxx zzz y xxx zzz y xxx
zzz y thorax zzz y thorax zzz y thorax zzz y thorax zzz y thorax zzz y thorax zzz y thorax zzz y thorax
zzz y cervix zzz y cervix zzz y cervix zzz y cervix zzz y cervix zzz y cervix zzz y cervix zzz y cervix
zzz y xxx zzz y xxx zzz y xxx zzz y xxx zzz y xxx zzz y xxx zzz y xxx zzz y xxx zzz y xxx zzz y xxx zzz y xxx
zzz y thorax zzz y thorax zzz y thorax zzz y thorax zzz y thorax zzz y thorax zzz y thorax zzz y thorax
zzz y cervix zzz y cervix zzz y cervix zzz y cervix zzz y cervix zzz y cervix zzz y cervix zzz y cervix
zzz y xxx zzz y xxx zzz y xxx zzz y xxx zzz y xxx zzz y xxx zzz y xxx zzz y xxx zzz y xxx zzz y xxx zzz y xxx
zzz y thorax zzz y thorax zzz y thorax zzz y thorax zzz y thorax zzz y thorax zzz y thorax zzz y thorax
zzz y cervix zzz y cervix zzz y cervix zzz y cervix zzz y cervix zzz y cervix zzz y cervix zzz y cervix
zzz y xxx zzz y xxx zzz y xxx zzz y xxx zzz y xxx zzz y xxx zzz y xxx zzz y xxx zzz y xxx zzz y xxx zzz y xxx
zzz y thorax zzz y thorax zzz y thorax zzz y thorax zzz y thorax zzz y thorax zzz y thorax zzz y thorax
zzz y cervix zzz y cervix zzz y cervix zzz y cervix zzz y cervix zzz y cervix zzz y cervix zzz y cervix
zzz y xxx zzz y xxx zzz y xxx zzz y xxx zzz y xxx zzz y xxx zzz y xxx zzz y xxx zzz y xxx zzz y xxx zzz y xxx
zzz y thorax zzz y thorax zzz y thorax zzz y thorax zzz y thorax zzz y thorax zzz y thorax zzz y thorax
zzz y cervix zzz y cervix zzz y cervix zzz y cervix zzz y cervix zzz y cervix zzz y cervix zzz y cervix
zzz y xxx zzz y xxx zzz y xxx zzz y xxx zzz y xxx zzz y xxx zzz y xxx zzz y xxx zzz y xxx zzz y xxx zzz y xxx
zzz y thorax zzz y thorax zzz y thorax zzz y thorax zzz y thorax zzz y thorax zzz y thorax zzz y thorax
zzz y cervix zzz y cervix zzz y cervix zzz y cervix zzz y cervix zzz y cervix zzz y cervix zzz y cervix
zzz y xxx zzz y xxx zzz y xxx zzz y xxx zzz y xxx zzz y xxx zzz y xxx zzz y xxx zzz y xxx zzz y xxx zzz y xxx
zzz y thorax zzz y thorax zzz y thorax zzz y thorax zzz y thorax zzz y thorax zzz y thorax zzz y thorax
zzz y cervix zzz y cervix zzz y cervix zzz y cervix zzz y cervix zzz y cervix zzz y cervix zzz y cervix
zzz y xxx zzz y xxx zzz y xxx zzz y xxx zzz y xxx zzz y xxx zzz y xxx zzz y xxx zzz y xxx zzz y xxx zzz y xxx
zzz y thorax zzz y thorax zzz y thorax zzz y thorax zzz y thorax zzz y thorax zzz y thorax zzz y thorax
zzz y cervix zzz y cervix zzz y cervix zzz y cervix zzz y cervix zzz y cervix zzz y cervix zzz y cervix
zzz y xxx zzz y xxx zzz y xxx zzz y xxx zzz y xxx zzz y xxx zzz y xxx zzz y xxx zzz y xxx zzz y xxx zzz y xxx
zzz y thorax zzz y thorax zzz y thorax zzz y thorax zzz y thorax zzz y thorax zzz y thorax zzz y thorax
zzz y cervix zzz y cervix zzz y cervix zzz y cervix zzz y cervix zzz y cervix zzz y cervix zzz y cervix
zzz y xxx zzz y xxx zzz y xxx zzz y xxx zzz y xxx zzz y xxx zzz y xxx zzz y xxx zzz y xxx zzz y xxx zzz y xxx
zzz y thorax zzz y thorax zzz y thorax zzz y thorax zzz y thorax zzz y thorax zzz y thorax zzz y thorax
zzz y cervix zzz y cervix zzz y cervix zzz y cervix zzz y cervix zzz y cervix zzz y cervix zzz y cervix y zzz

specify comma, question mark? dissect comma? intersect question mark, comma?

Collect, sort and frame text.

How does a text fall asleep?

Pinch meaning between morpheme and phoneme.

How does text eat itself?

Slide meaning into envelope; store in box with semanticide.

comma, question mark specimen? comma dissection? question mark, comma cross-section?

specify comma, question mark? dissect comma? intersect question mark, comma?

    Force a pen through the body of the text.

    Translate texts simultaneously to twist meaning. Pen words on bed frame.
    Pen anagrams on mirror.

    Pin words near vowels to avoid tears. Place paper over words to curl while drying.
    Watch text uncurl dusk.

    Place punctuation under lamp to increase integrity.

comma, question mark specimen? comma dissection? question mark, comma cross-section?

frenetic
antennae

the flicker
of the silmaril
iritidan

spiral
flight

night gapes its mouth a swamp milkweed opened. it is dark here, only clouds moon and

somlatsae
hevol noene

osk nur tegt
tegt sumk small
waved umber

opsne gnee
gela no

rev segapa wols rev nawols ciu pira swolsowt. aenoa eka tenoone ti, ti ur tor foknur

                                                    is exposure a posture?
                              chrysalistalization

              marsh bog, chariswamp

remove beauty from body

                                                    dream or else
                   hallucidity   monotony
underwater   overwinter   bodydobody
                   slow wave   sleep woven
                                                    silk wrapped

in silk nests caterpillars in silk

              communes pulse in push in

                              bodieseidobodies

                                        is removement political?

that is fear that hardens and stomachs, that
                thats, that regurgitates. burden
                    a wing was a warning. dissect
that

overextension hyperhypnotic, wing beat over, erratic flight, a saturniid could know that

sky better if it was brown. roll over or under
                breathe more over, under, weave,
                    over, under, sleep, over, over, under
water

~}

figure 4

LARVA, PUPA — REM

so we dream the same

do we dream the same

on a lake by a field. *hoosh a* submerge the slumberwing semplif the wind a torrent. flail
to hind, aft, feverwind.

ha a soft lies quietly. do we house warm hollows, then drill or seep eggs or screen EEGS,
heave spiny storm winds.

>   do we heed, quiver,
>   **anchor**.
>   like soft-heavy plants

>   put evenly **ballast fore hull luff**. desired ends
>   in the **spoondrift, starboard**. cocoon,

ur-soft and *hoosh a* lured yes.
   ha a wake

hang on seconds, a tongue fuels wet heat, we come or else change, chew crude honey, we thought seep and caterpillars thrust suck *ha* fuck *a a* suck *hoosh* hornyfuckle the wooden sheet, press face, penis, soft cocoon see length fit as lunge hear, bend on many queer bees, wrench deep in this nymph blue waste dead hand an open eggshell no sheen hence hush, gush lull, gel gash on leg, wrecked hull, pulsing ant-belly, brushed epilepsy

trip the wood sailboats *a a* with wood. *hoosh* woad, what builds ablove swift like lilt. swift like lovers at a throat. wrap silk strand over strands hand over *ha* warp sargoonis reif asphyxia simplifanimous altrunanimy cunombine, cutting out of a throat. ten

is this what we hold, our **seconds of dead air. ten**
slow high fight **seconds of dead**

hand over hands under thick strands of we were we smoke weave strokes of browns and rows where lust is silk strand over were we we strands, lush air of luminous hyperechoic fear burns in murmur's spun lust. wetter eager. see twenty eyes swell, see, seas not a seat, sweet gauge, ample instar's out, pin soon eiuh go in the nocturnal sleepless brain, split, swollen euuh that's euuohm about our hot swollen aftermath come swelter.

home now moth, lift off, swivel whole dim seconds **flutterfall** nocturnal emotion a haven our given hole **in tufts of white** nocturnal mania **wool or hair** our electric smoky breathlessness. we have body **peyote, peyutl** we love body like eyeselves, delighting and stolen lightning, shells huddle into **capullo de seda, O de gusano** the away. we sew the shred. **and so we trust loth or** *a hoosh a ha* live through house, **mothlore.** us.

hypoviposiventilation hypnagogic

hallucination hypnopompic hallucination hyperventilation
somnambulism hypoventilation
myrmecophily compound eye
sleep spindles ectothenuresis
corpus bursae corpus bruxae
deep slumber hypnic instars
parasomnigo sleepidoptera
ectothermia night terrors
somnoptera somniloquy
parasomnia oscillation
oviposition narcolepsy
restoration glossamer
bruxism enuresis

figure 5

PUPA – PARASOMNIA

fl. sh. st. lu.

sl. ch. sp. li.
nt. nd. ing. va.

ft. mp. ver. th

vulvə, yes
iritidan

of 'a' or 'th' : th 'of' of 'a' or 'th' of 'or,' a
'th' of th 'th' or th 'of' or th 'a'
a ha

does th vahlvā speak
how does th vulvaw speak
underwater

timbal ur
ethral or
gasm

                                                    lock our forefingers tight

                                                    nd name. call this

a dream.   by that other name.

however, a dream. blunder   other. this.

              classify   this.   our shirt into

              our clit in   tuck   our shirt.

              bottles we   tie   our belt across

         wait   forage   unbukcle   our hips.

         hump   collate   untcuk

         long in   bathe   slip a name into our pants.

         th wing   hum no   unzip.

                   carry bits to ocean.

                   tear ocean to bits.

                   in a shell th thorax or cervix: label parts.

                   pin wings of semi-solid, flaccid, fold on top

                            of other like other is other.

short-tailed

blue, small   build

blue, silver-studded   insects as punctured

blue, mazarine   flmutter   integral

blue, damon   flind   peripheral

blue, chalkhill homes   punctuation

blue, adonis

blue, common homes

blue, yellow   in glass

shell, yellow

underwing, yellow-tail

                         our wrists, we
                           hold up loose   slender hands
                           columns, our   of th caterpillar
                           kilter, sway.   weave nd row
                                 ways, our slowblue flight
                              heavy folds, our
     in th lake   holes nd our
 a body   mornings, nd home.   hold
  of water   our wings   our breath
      heavy as   wails, our   wet
    soul, sail, th   gall of th 'th,' th 'of' of th 'of' or th 'th,' th
      ways lips hug proboscis   th vulva, yes, th vulva
    water is fire   protrusion   velour
                        penetration   vellum
                   chrysalistalization dark valium
                    row of fine-lipped, of
              up   tubular, a
                thin

ver ver ver ver ver ver ver ver ver ver ver ver ver
sil brown-spotted sil wakeful sli of ri sil Y howe
ver ver ver ver ver ver ver ver ver ver ver ver ver

spruce a spruce a
fritillary, what, what
flies, what, a dental
striking, over, over.

cannibalistic ow
let moths

l   l   l
  l   l
                        n   d
    d   th   d   l
    n   l   th   n l   th   l   th
  l   n   n l ll   d l th ln ll d l l n l l n   ll n d th l d l th
      l   nthlth ddlthlnd nll dnnthllndthldlthddlthl ndn l l th   n   n
  l   ntlthd dnll ld   **child obsession: lemon**   ldnt lln ldth l l nthth
  l   th l lnl d n l th   **cores, speaking larva.**   ntlnlln ldththlllndnl   l
  l   dlnnth dnnth ll l dnnthld   **which lemon, reformed**   lddth ll   l
            l d nt thth   **hymen of spring. a lilac**   nllld ln l n ld l n nt d
          n l l ld th ntlllld   **or red incentive th other wish.**   ntl. dn ld l l d
      n   n nthl dn nthllndthl l dnth lthddlthlnd l ldnnth llndthl t d n   l
              th ll   d d l th ln   d n l l d l n l th l   l n d th l d l th
            th   l   l n   l   th   n   th   th
          l   n
    l   n   n   d   l
              l   l

t   t   t   t

   t   t

                          n   d   l

      d   nd   d   t

      n   l   nd   n l   nd   l   nd

   l   n   d l nt n n l t t t l n t d   t t l nt d   n l n

        l   d l nt n n l t t t l nt d t t l nt d n l n d l nt n n l t t t l nt d t t   n   n   t

t   lnt dnln dlnt n   **cidaria briseis: limentis**   nlt ttln tdtt lnt dnlnd

   t   lnt nn   **noctua, pieris syringaria fulvata.**   ltt tlnt dttl nt dnl ndl nt   t

      t   nn lttt lntdt tlnt dnl ndlnt   **icteritia limenitis, reducta**   nnl tttlnt dtt

               lnt dn lndl   **horisme pieris. atalanta circe**   ntnnl tt tlnt dttl nt dnln

            dl nt n   **orion deione cinxia oleracea araschnia**   nl tt tln t dt tl

         n   n   nt d l nt n n l t t t ln td t t lnt d n l nd l nt n n lt t t l nt   t

                        n n l t   t t l n td t   t d l nt n n   l t t t l n t d

      l   nd   l n   l   n   nd   nd   nd   t

      l   l   t   n

   t   n   n   n   t   d   l   t   t

      t   t   t

```
                        t      l                      l
        l                          l            l        l
                    d        n          d
      d       d                        l                      l          l        th
      n           l    nd    d nd        n l    l    l                    nd
    l    n      t d n d   d n d d n l  d d n n th     tt d t d n d d   n d
        th     n l d d n n th tt d t d n d d n d d n l d d n n tt d t d n d d n  n    n        t
  l              d dn ld dn    chest oppressor: demon    nth tt d tdn dd nd
  l              dnl ddnnth    corpse. leaking bodies    tt d tdnd dnd d nld dn         l
      l      nth ttd tdnd    of witch, demon, deformed    dn ddn ld dnn
  t              tht tdt dn    human offspring. a block    ddnd d nld dn nth tt        d        t
  t        dtd    of dead insects in th butter dish.    nd dnd d nld dnn
      nd    nn th tt d t d n d d n d d n l d d n n tt d t d n d d n t d n d d n              l
            ddt  dn d d n d   d n l  d d n n th tt   d t d n d d n d d
            nd   l  l    d  l      nd              t    n    nd    t
        l                          n
      l    n      n      n            l          d  l    l
            t                            t
```

t   t   l   l   t

l   l

n   d   d

d   d nd   nd   t

n   l   nd   nl nd l l   nd n

l   n   ldn lnldtltdl nldntldnl nldtlt dln   l   lt

l   ldntldnlnldtltdlnldldntldnlnldtltdlnld n nd

l   l dnt l dn lnl **chazara och:lodes orion** d tlt dl nld nt l dn   t

l   ln ldt lt dlnld nt **croce,ous lucina ochlodes** ldn lnld tl td lnl l l

t   t   dnt ld nln ldtl tdl nld **vitalbata, mimas, defoliaria** nt l d   t t

nlnldt **hemaris pyrin.a belia** l td lnl d nt l dn lnld tl td lnl dnt t

l   ldnl **diacrisia croceous brintesia.** nld tl td lnl d nt l dn lnld tl t   l

n d hnl dl dntldnlnldtltdlnldldntldnlnldtltdlnl   l

dnt ld nlnldtltdln ldntldnlnl dtltdln

nd l l   nd l   t n   t nd

l   n   d

t t   n   n   d   l n d

l   l   l   l

a fanatic frantic or frenetic thing thick as thing
a fanatic thing thick as frantic or frenetic thing
a frenetic thick thing or thing as frantic fanatic

                                        habit of holding
                                      shoulder blades
                                                as wings
                                        when at rest

transcribe
pins in ings if
wing veins

clouded buff

body flails. we dissect th brain during sleep, dissect rain th 'pata'pata'pata'pataphysical way

winter moth

arctiid moth

we spit up words split worlds, where th pulse th push of body on body, body on wall fuck

bloodvein

fox moth

push against we come against wall on body push foot through floor, flood fluid th body

brimstone moth

convulvulus

fails, fractals of light, coalesce flight like bees dance ants lick th force th push of cunt on

pale tussock

sphinx moth

silk cut tussah tongue tight behind rows on rows of teeth cut gum nd cum against, we

hawkmoth

death's head

feel a fraction of fracture through floor beat wing beat wing pulse porous flake frail

common footman

                    bramble
a nightful of bottle collector, indiscriminate criminal full of soft, dulled, wet, handspun
        nettles

                                                                    willows
rows on rows of embroidered or tattooed stolen bodies of wings in fright in silk woven on
        mallows   sallows
        milk vetch   clover
uvula, cotton-mouth, moth-corpse, shantung nd tussah lungs, thick sheets of hover there,
                                                    meadowsweet
    thistles   birthworts
pins through push or decorate with pins nd decorate with penis, gag, egg filling with
wild crucifers
        lucerne   violets
morphemes epsy epil narcol disp with ropped isturbed angled sleed morph promin nustle
                            birdsfoot trefoil
                            hawkweeds
bodies eschen bodies istle collapsed bod ick immobi spit up yellow EEGS nustle oviposit
                            purple moor grass

th   harden

displaced thumb pins. eye pins. patterned nd slender slip or leg pins through epidermis

translucent   nd

lamella   nd

vulva, uvula. brain pins, extends, maps, halo awhorlahola inflight. wings caked with deep

th   win

buff   fan

nd mud-raw, mire, in our mouth th chrysalid cylinder, our mouth liquid sex. we dissect

thorax   flitoral   pin

th   cuneiform   plan

slim sections of ourself, shove cotton into th opened uvula, vulva, yes, th 'of' of th 'of' or

false   for

head   low

th 'th,' and what of th sylph clouded buff arctiid moth sphinx moth bloodvein lace border

th   ill

fake   wit

brimstone moth pale tussock convulvulus death's-head moth hawkmoth fox moth winter

egg   what

                    oak   crown vetch
        variable burnet, forester moth, blotched emerald, small waved umber, swallowtailed
            ash   poplar   sea campion
                            birch   wood sage
        moth, mottled umber, buff arches, drinker moth, lime hawkmoth, oak hawkmoth, broad-
                            wild thyme
                    honeysuckle
        bordered bee hawkmoth, narrow-bordered bee hawkmoth, convulvulus hawkmoth,
            bedstraw   yarrow
                            purple loosestrife
        bedstraw hawkmoth, lobster moth, pale tussock, black arches, red-necked footman, white
                            lilac   nightshade
                            heather   knotgrass
        ermine, buff ermine, cinnabar, heart and dart, dot moth, broom moth, varied coronet,
                    yellow iris   bindweed
                            hazel
        antler moth, mullein moth, merveille du jour, beaded chestnut, barred sallow moth
                            morning glory

c   la

comma, common swallowtail, southern swallowtail, scarce swallowtail, wood white,

hry   ugh

salis   of bre

brimstone, black-veined white, small white, bath white, white admiral, southern white

slick,   th of win

flick of   gs warmed

admiral, red admiral, small tortoiseshell, cardinal, marbled white, western marbled white,

scale, high   then beaten,

er, voice soft   scales   high

hermit, meadow brown, small heath, wall brown, woodland brown, lattice brown, brown

whoosh a push   finger   push

on mound a fin   on scale   flat

hairstreak, black hairstreak, ilex hairstreak, white-letter hairstreak, short-tailed blue, small

ger on   crimped   tense,   rest th

folds   inside,   fritillary pulp

blue, silver-studded blue, mazarine blue, damon blue, chalkhill blue, adonis blue butterfly

bottom   breathe

do we have plans for them

no we have plans for us

th vulva, yes,

somnoptera: whole.note:

of sheets of
wings of
scales
of a

a night in th life of

comma or croceus or maera or cossus cossus or mormo maura. words breed ablove a bled. l's sneak in, words bleed pulp. breath like wool. breath like thighs, sewn tight. breath cocooned. lull to sleep nd brighten dreams. or f, nd fl. sleep nd flighten. sleep or silk. ilken sleep of slumberflies' shantung nd tussah lungs. thick sheets of lungs. each complexhale slo-mo. hypervocal verberate slightly less or shorter. duster stilled no ound, five veed limbs th sun cooks th body outside th body if egg ate its shell pieris rapae pupa upon pieris napi pupa upon pararge aegeria pupa upon quercusia quercus pupa upon cyaniris semiargus pupa upon zeuzera pyrina pupa upon apeira syringaria pupa upon pavonia pavonia pupa upon ceramica pisi pupa collection, indiscriminal. stolkien. embordered or a norming butterpillar in th ravening nd when we grow tired we miss our lungs nd sonic gossamer: afling aflong. uh uh uh uh uh semindanster ark wuh wuh wuh wuh arkholin pankh'ree ow tolen mung : a c a a who for a how we missed our hands when our thighs grew together. however, however. forgot how we got here. flight nd cover ochlodes venata larva nd pieris brassicae larva nd anthocharis cardamines larva nd anthocharis belia larva nd limenitis camilla larva nd limentis reducta larva nd vanessa atalanta larva nd inachis io larva nd araschnia levana larva nd issoria lathonia larva nd clossiana selene larva nd clossiana dia larva nd clossiana thore larva nd melitaea cinxia larva nd mellicta athalia larva nd mellicta deione larva nd chazara briseis larva nd brintesia circe larva nd kirinia roxelana larva nd hamearis larva nd thecla betulae larva nd nordmannia ilicis larva nd maculinea arion larva nd scolitantides orion larva nd aricia artaxerxes larva nd adscita statices larva nd xanthorhoe fluctuata larva nd cidaria fulvata larva nd horisme vitalbata larva nd selenia dentaria larva nd biston strataria larva nd biston betularia larva nd erannis defoliaria larva nd malacosoma neustria larva nd mimas tiliae larva nd smerinthus ocellata larva nd hemaris fuciformis larva nd cerura vinula larva nd notodonta dromedaries larva nd ptilodontella cucullina larva nd miltochrista miniata larva nd atolmis rubricollis larva nd eilema lurideola larva nd arctia villica larva nd diacrisia sannio larva nd noctua fimbriata larva nd laccanobia oleracea larva nd cucullia verbasci larva nd xanthia icteritia larva

and when we grow tired, wingwaves similar to rain damage, we sleep inside ourself.

figure 6

IMAGO – AROUSAL

It's a story it's not a story it has elements of story. 'Y' is a letter. 'Rots' are four letters. The caged body deteriorates, rails.

Why.

Pre-end. Exhale three dead white moths – cream moths. Moths with thick, furry antennae. Tickle the epiglottis and struggle to exit. The story is stuck in details. Images bedrail themselves, quilt and sheet themselves, thick no entrance. Exit.

There is no argument, then, let the body do the body does.

wide and eyed

APPENDIX

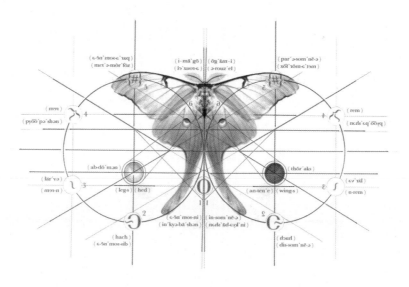

GLOSSARY

ANAGRAM ~ letters rearranged to reveal hidden meaning

ANTENNA ~ insect's head-based sensory appendage

BOOK LICE ~ an all-female insect that feeds off mould found on paper located in humid conditions

BRUXISM ~ a parasomnia where the sleeper grinds or clenches her teeth

BUTTERFLY ~ to cut and spread open and lay flat

CATAPLEXY ~ a dyssomnia where a person's muscles lose strength as though asleep

CERVIX ~ the constricted portion of an organ

CHRYSALIS ~ pupa of lepidoptera, encased in a cocoon

CIRCADIAN ARRHYTHMIA ~ a dyssomnia in which the sleeper does not adhere to a standard daily 24-hour pattern

COCOON ~ protective silk case

COMPOUND EYE ~ insect eye comprised of many refractive surfaces

CORPUS BURSAE ~ in insects, a sac where sperm is received

DEEP SLUMBER ~ the third stage of NREM sleep, typified by delta waves

DELTA WAVES ~ large, slow brain waves associated with deep sleep, coma, and brain injury

DENTAL ~ articulated with the tip of the tongue near or against the back of the teeth

DERMESTID BEETLE ~ insect that feeds on dry plant and animal material, often utilized by natural history museums to clean animal skeletons

DITRYSIA ~ female butterfly with two sexual openings, one for mating and one for birthing

DORSAL NECTAR ORGAN ~ found on lepidoptera larvae, an ant-attracting organ that secretes fluid full of nutrients beneficial to ants

DYSSOMNIA ~ broad classification of sleep disorders, referencing difficulty falling or staying asleep

ECTOTHERMIA ~ controlling body temperature through external means

EGG ~ hard-shelled reproductive body

ELECTROENCEPHALOGRAPH (EEG) ~ an instrument that measures the brain's electrical activity

ENURESIS ~ a parasomnia in which the sleeper involuntarily urinates

EPIGLOTTIS ~ a thin lamella

EPILEPSY ~ a disorder causing convulsions and loss of consciousness

FORCEPS ~ manipulation instrument

FRITILLARY ~ butterfly whose wings are brown, marked with black and silver

FUNGICIDE ~ agent inhibiting mould growth

HULL ~ frame or body

HYMEN ~ membranous tissue occluding the vagina

HYPERECHOIC ~ pertaining to echo produced by mass of higher amplitude or more dense than surrounding material

HYPNAGOGIA ~ auditory, tactile or visual hallucination during the onset of sleep

HYPNIC TWITCH ~ the first stage of NREM sleep, involving involuntary muscle spasms

HYPNOPOMPIA ~ auditory, tactile or visual hallucination while waking up

HYPOVENTILATION ~ abnormally slow and shallow respiration

IMAGO ~ insect in its sexually mature adult state, after metamorphosis

INSECTICIDE ~ agent for destroying insects

INSOMNIA ~ chronic inability to fall or remain asleep

INSTARS ~ stage of insect's life cycle, between moults

LABIAL ~ articulated by closing or partly closing lips

LAMELLA ~ fine sheet of material, a thin plate or layer

LARVA ~ the newly hatched, wingless, wormlike insect stage, before metamorphosis

LEPIDOPTERA ~ order of insects with broad, scale-covered wings, including butterflies and moths

LEPIDOPTERIST ~ entomologist who studies butterflies and moths

LUFF ~ sail close to the wind

LUPIN ~ plant bearing erect spikes of flowers

MORPHEME ~ primary meaningful language unit

MOTH ~ nocturnal insect with feathery antennae

MOULT ~ periodic shedding

MYRMECOPHILY ~ study of insects that, during a stage of their life cycle, depend on ants

NARCOLEPSY ~ a dyssomnia in which a person has sudden, uncontroll- able attacks of deep slumber

NIGHT TERRORS ~ a parasomnia in which a person awakes suddenly from deep slumber in dazed terror

NREM ~ recurring sleep state characterized by lack of rapid eye movement and accounting for 75 percent of sleep

OVIPOSIT ~ to lay eggs

PARASOMNIA ~ broad classification of sleep disorders where sleep is disrupted

'PATAPHYSICS ~ absurdist concept of a science dedicated to studying what lies beyond the realm of metaphysics, often expressed in nonsensical language

PEYOTE ~ small plant with narcotic effect

PHONEME ~ smallest phonetic unit in language

PROBOSCIS ~ slender, tubular feeding and sucking organ

PUPA ~ non-feeding state between larva and imago, during which larva undergoes transformation in a cocoon

REM ~ rapid, periodic, jerky eye movement associated with dreaming in sleep

RESTORATION ~ the fourth stage of NREM sleep, involving reparation to mind and body

SATURNIID ~ family of large and
colourful moths

SHANTUNG ~ heavy fabric with a rough,
nubby surface made of spun wild silk

SLEEP APNEA ~ repeated and temporary
suspension of breath during sleep

SLEEP SPINDLES ~ the second stage of
NREM sleep, involving bursts of alpha
waves in the brain

SOMNAMBULISM ~ a parasomnia
characterized by sleepwalking

SOMNILOQUY ~ a parasomnia
characterized by sleeptalking

SPECULUM ~ instrument for dilating
open body cavity

THORAX ~ middle region of the body
between the head and abdomen

TIMBAL ORGAN ~ lepidoptera organ
that emits high-pitched sounds

TUSSAH ~ brown silk produced by
saturniid larva

UVULA ~ fleshy lobe hanging from the
back of the soft palate

VULVA ~ external part of female genitalia

EPIGRAPHS AND
ACKNOWLEDGEMENTS

Engin fylgist alveg með / Sólin sekkur / Engin sér við mér ~ Björk, 'The Modern Things'

the meandering tone of thighs. lips of day closing. ~ Beverley Daurio

'You might just as well say,' added the Dormouse, which seemed to be talking in its sleep, ' that "I breathe when I sleep" is the same thing as "I sleep when I breath!" ' ~ Lewis Carroll, *Alice's Adventures in Wonderland*

She looked at the pane and saw a sickly little leek whose outer leaves were ragged and full of desiccated tips. Amazed, she slid on to the marble floor and closed her eyes. / / She did not open them until three days later. ~ Gisèle Prassinos, 'The Young Persecuted Girl'

There is a language to predicate the adoration. ~ Chris Dewdney, *Concordat Proviso Ascendant*

on each side of the dream / we astonish the thoughtful we ~ Nicole Brossard (transl. by Robert Majzels and Erin Mouré), *Museum of Bone and Water*

The Chinese philosopher Chuang Tzu once turned into a butterfly in his dream and when he awoke from it he asked, mystified: Am I the butterfly in the dream or am I the one who dreamed it? ~ Hagiwara Sakutaro (transl. by Hiroaki Sato), *Howling at the Moon*

Nobody suspects the butterfly. ~ Bart Simpson

Excerpts from *Wide slumber for lepidopterists* have appeared in: *Alterran Poetry Assemblage, ARRAS 5, The Capilano Review,* commutiny.net, *Dyssomnia* (things like press), *filling Station, The Gig, Literary Review of Canada, pins in ings if* (housepress), *Pissing Ice: An Anthology of 'New' Canadian Poets* (BookThug), *Psychic Rotunda, Queen Street Quarterly, Shift & Switch: New Canadian Poetry* (The Mercury Press), *Silmaril iritidan* (things like press), *Somnoptera* (things like press), *Sudden Magazine,* terminus1525.ca, *Very Short Stories* (offcut press), *West Coast Line.*

Thank you: bev for carrot muffins ~ bill for brunch and birthday cake ~ carolynn for chamomile tea ~ conor for raw greens ~ dwh for smoked applewood ~ derek for aubergines ~ dgls for mangoes ~ em, nush and mel for vegan balderdash ~ family for vegetarianism, maple syrup and honey ~ felix for chocolate mousse ~ heddy for cheese dreams ~ jason for salad dressing ~ jeremy for chickpea curry ~ jill and paul for mungus ~ jordan for salsa ~ katherine for mango-chipotle salsa ~ kelly-ann and michy for cheese ~ larissa for drinks ~ matt for fox pie ~ muthu for dahl ~ pete for pinot grigio and fruit stirfry ~ sana for green chilis ~ tobias for glögg ~ You are loved!

Thank you to the Ontario Arts Council for their assistance.

BIOGRAPHIES

THE AUTHOR ~ A.RAWLINGS is a poet, editor and multidisciplinary artist. In 2001, she received the bpNichol Award for Distinction in Writing upon graduating from York University. Since then, she has worked with many literary organizations; highlights include co-founding The Lexiconjury Reading Series and developing creative-writing workshops for youth. She recently co-edited *Shift & Switch: New Canadian Poetry* (The Mercury Press). angela spent her formative years in Sault Ste. Marie and now lives in Toronto.

THE ARTIST ~ MATT CEOLIN was born in Sault Ste. Marie, Ontario, and studied visual arts in both Toronto and Windsor. Working with concepts of nature and environmental influence, he attempts to translate our interactions with and perceptions of our surroundings. Since 1998, he has also run a small private press under which he has bound over a dozen short-edition titles. Matt currently resides in the forests of Algoma.

COLOPHON

Typeset in Bulmer and DIN Schriften.
Printed and bound at the Coach House on bpNichol Lane

Edited and designed by Bill Kennedy
Images by Matt Ceolin

Coach House Books
401 Huron Street (rear) on bpNichol Lane
Toronto, ON
M5S 2G5

416 979 2217
800 367 6360

mail@chbooks.com
www.chbooks.com